A Triumph of Restora

Oxford Rewley Road Statio

Lance Adlam and Bill Simpson

Lamplight Publications

Published by Lamplight Publications
260 Colwell Drive,
Witney,
Oxon
OX28 5LW

First Published 2008

ISBN: 978-1-899246-21-2

Printed and bound at
The Alden Press,
De Havilland Way,
Witney,
Oxon
OX29 0YG

Contents

The station seen during the second World War. Note that the panels below the window sills were still timber cladding, throughout, they were later changed to brick (see p 29 of 1951).

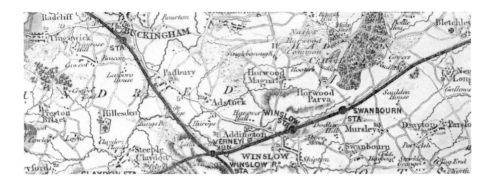

An Outline of the History of the Buckinghamshire Railway

It is strange how a proposal can be changed by some local event in history that can bring about a series of circumstances that alter plans and bring about quite a different outcome. This leaves the historian forever pondering how things would have developed if these original plans had been realised Such an event, was the financial collapse of the local bank at Aylesbury called Medleys.

Between 1833 - 1838 the London & Birmingham Railway was under construction passing east of Aylesbury by about seven miles. The merchants hoped that it would pass through the town but land owning interests at the time had supported alternative investment in the construction of the Aylesbury Branch of the Grand Junction Canal and they were not disposed to see this happen. The merchant businessmen of Aylesbury had already been frustrated by the dilatory way the the canal had reached the town as late as 1814. They were determined that the same would not happen in the case of the railway.

A group of business men formed the Aylesbury Railway Company on November 12, 1834 to connect with the London & Birmingham main line near the village of Cheddington. Canal interests opposed this new branch line but could not stop it becoming law and it received the Royal Assent on May 19, 1836.

The London & Birmingham Railway, supported the Aylesbury Railway but were not simply interested in reaching that town. They viewed things much further afield. They had watched warily as the newly formed Great Western Railway advanced up the Thames Valley heading west towards Bristol. Both companies viewed the territory between them as ripe for the advancement of their own systems.

An example of this was the Cheltenham, Oxford & London & Birmingham Union Railway. This was to have a junction at Tring and the line was at first planned to pass through Aylesbury and have a branch from it to Oxford. Had

The situation in the Thames Valley area in 1845. Note the dotted lines of proposed railways: to Oxford from north London; and more importantly from Aylesbury.

Bill Simpson Collection

things remained thus it is quite possible that this would have been the main line to Oxford in 1839. However, Robert Stephenson decided that this was not the most economical route and drew plans that came no closer to Aylesbury than Bishopstone. This would not do for the sponsors of the Aylesbury Railway who had been asked to support the new scheme and they withdrew their support for the CO&L&BU scheme that then could not raise enough capital to continue.

For the Aylesbury Railway proprietors this left them with the possibility of extending their line to Oxford with a terminus on the east side of the River Cherwell, in the area known as St Clements.

This was where the financial crisis revised the plans. The local financial support for the Aylesbury Railway came from the Aylesbury bank of Medley's. This collapsed in January 1837 before the line had even begun construction. The Aylesbury directors called a special meeting to consider whether they were now able to fulfil their commitments to the line. They must have been very keen for it to proceed as the scheme was now a far greater financial risk. Would it successfully compete with the canal? Would mechanical shortcomings, breakdowns etc, cause a loss of faith in the new line? The railways were still very much at the experimental stage in operating, even with the massive investment that the L&BR had undertaken.

In the event it was decided to go ahead with the line to Aylesbury but to shelve a planned extension to Oxford. Had this not happened then it is likely that the railway would have been looking to open a line in that city by 1840-1, three years before the broad gauge line from Didcot, by the Oxford Railway and their station in Grandpont, much further from the city centre than the Aylesbury line station had planned to be.

The first sod was cut for the Aylesbury Railway on May 12, 1838 some five months before completion of the L&B main line; the line was opened on June 10, 1839 as a single line but with the possibility of future extension, space was reserved for another set of rails.

The London & Birmingham Railway was now completed and was gaining connections to the East Midlands at Rugby, but still looked westwards for future expansion.

The L&B supported interest in two lines projected through the north of Buckinghamshire and Oxfordshire. These were the Buckingham & Brackley Junction Railway, for a line from Bletchley near Fenny Stratford to Buckingham and Brackley, and secondly another scheme, for a line to have a junction near Claydon through Bicester to Oxford: the Oxford & Bletchley Railway. The L&B were most concerned to reach Banbury in their pursuit of the West Midlands.

The construction of the line to Oxford that eventually had a terminus on the site of Rewley Abbey (Rewley Road) would have been very doubtful if the Cheddington or Tring schemes had been fully realised. Consequently the station building that was eventually moved from the Oxford site in 1999 would never have existed.

Both schemes had been promoted in 1845 and a year later the L&BR became part of a much larger concern, the London & North Western Railway formed in 1846. The L&NWR was just as interested in expanding their network to Cheltenham and the West Midlands and advised the two companies to form a single company called the Buckinghamshire Railway, and that they would finance extending the line from Brackley to Banbury.

By now the GWR having opened in Oxford in 1844 were advancing north to, first of all Rugby, later this was changed to Birmingham, Banbury was the point of intersection for them both. With the LNWR line opening there on May 1st 1850, whilst the GWR opened there in September 1850.

The GWR had to resort to taking the L&NWR to the Court of Chancery to enforce legal agreements previously entered with the L&NWR which allowed the GWR to continue to carry its line north to Birmingham and the LNWR remained with their 'temporary' timber terminus at Banbury.

The line to Oxford from Claydon (Verney Junction) was extended to reach Islip on October 1, 1850 and Banbury Road on December 2nd, 1850. After some manoeuvring of various schemes it reached a temporary terminus at Oxford Road, a few miles north of Oxford, on December 20, 1850, finally opening in the city on May 20, 1851.

The citizens of Oxford had been complaining about both existing 'temporary' stations (Grandpont and Oxford Road) for some time. At that time the GWR passed by the station site but remained south of the river until 1852 when a new through station was built with an overall roof. The station of the Buckinghamshire Railway was far less conventional and very remarkable. Events leading to its construction are part of constructional engineering history.

The former GWR (1852) station was overdue for rebuilding prior to World War Two. Reconstruction eventually came in 1971 and was still woefully inadequate for Oxford with its constantly travelling university population. Twenty years later the present station was built which is a big improvement on what was there before. At the time of writing (December 2007) there are proposals for a completely new station on the south side of the Botley Road bridge which will give more platforms and through lines to ease the Oxford station bottleneck that currently exists.

The Oxford (Rewley Road) station of the Buckinghamshire Railway was in inevitable decline from the ending of its passengers services in 1951. Indeed the company that took it all over in 1923, the London Midland & Scottish Railway made arrangements with the GWR in the 1930's for their stationmaster to manage the LMS station and yards as well. They already shared the goods shed from an historical agreement.

The LMS showed the station buildings little maintenance attention apart from changing the signs and some paintwork. A photograph is included showing it in the 1940's which shows how shabby its appearance had become although the LMS must have appreciated the considerable coal revenues from the yard that was always well stocked.

In 1966 the large timber goods shed and several sections of the station building were demolished. The drift of general goods to the road was well under way with the opening of the new motorways from 1956 onwards to the present day and the 'smalls' traffic declined.

The Station site at Oxford

The site at Oxford was land that had been occupied from 1287 by the modest structure of the Cistercian Abbey of Rewley. Following the dissolution of the monasteries in 1536 land was eventually passed by King Henry VIII to Christ Church in 1545. The College removed stones for other structures from the ruin of Rewley Abbey which seems to have had a long history of being used as a quarry for other buildings following the dissolution. In 1537 King Henry VIII removed 40 windows for use in his Hampton Court Palace bowling alley, and the lead from the roof was used to cover the Queen's New Gallery.

The area served as gardens for fresh produce, no doubt for the colleges, whilst the remaining buildings were later used for a brew house (1725). Some of the ruins must have remained long enough for the organist of Magdalen College,

Mr R Parrett to sell them off for the building of the Lady Chapel of St Mary Magdalen Church

In May 1849. Part of the site was sold to the Great Western Railway as the site for their new station opened in 1852. The remainder including the buildings was sold to the Buckinghamshire Railway in1851 for their new station.

If you imagine the station sites before construction the ground level was part of the flood plain at no more than about two feet (60 cm) above the level of the existing 'Sheepwash Channel', the connection between the Oxford Canal (which arrived in 1795) and the River Thames. The canal, required the railway company to strike a level to give clear headway over the canal. This was achieved by building a swing bridge.

The GWR of course had to strike good levels to cross the

Thames from Grandpont, so that was already part of their survey and construction proposal. To bridge the canal in the same way with such a low level of the ground would have required the Buckinghamshire Railway to raise their embankment to give suitable clearance for the canal users. Such a construction would have had major ramifications for the line and future station levels which already had approximately 8 feet depth of filling material spread over the Rewley Road station site.

The Buckinghamshire Railway had promoted its scheme during the financial panic of 1847 and much of the works that had already been completed had been the barest minimum necessary to pass Board of Trade standards. In that year the company halted work on the line to Oxford to concentrate on the line to Brackley and Banbury because of a shortage of funds.

There were complaints that the station at Buckingham was a mean wooden building. It would be some ten years later, probably as funds allowed, before this structure was replaced with the one that echoed the classical grandeur of nearby Stowe, notwithstanding that this was the station for one of the leading proponents of the line, the Duke of Buckingham!

There is every good reason to believe that the first station at Claydon, for the Chairman of the line, Sir Harry Verney was also rather more basic than it subsequently became.

What can be deduced from the financial strictures imposed on the directors was that the Buckinghamshire Railway would be able to open its line and whilst they would probably have liked to have something imposing at Oxford they would have to look for the simplest cost effective structure. What did become available came as a result of the building for the 'Great Exhibition of Works of Industry of all Nations: 1851' which had been designed by Sir Joseph Paxton. Details of the station structure are to follow in subsequent chapters, so sufficient at this point to mention its origins.

The Contractors who developed Paxton's design and produced the working drawings and engineering expertise for constructing the Exhibition Building parts were Fox, Henderson & Co of Stafford, who were well known to the LNWR board members and were in contact through moving parts of the Exhibition building from the Black Country southwards by rail to London (Euston). Other parts also came to London by canal.

Engineers Charles Fox (1810-1874) and John Henderson entered partnership from 1841 until 1856, when their firm collapsed. At their liquidation Fox, Henderson owed £320,000 and laid off some 2000 workers.

Fox was a pupil of Robert Stephenson on the building of the London & Birmingham Railway and designed the original train shed roof at Euston in 1837. He was also responsible for Birkenhead Market (1845). A cast iron lighthouse for India (1850). And worked on Paddington station with Brunel and Sir Matthew Digby Wyatt (1850-4). The Great Exhibition Building (Crystal Palace) with Sir Joseph Paxton (1850), Oxford Station of the LNWR (1851); Birmingham New Street station with Couper (1852-4) and the Kiev suspension bridge.

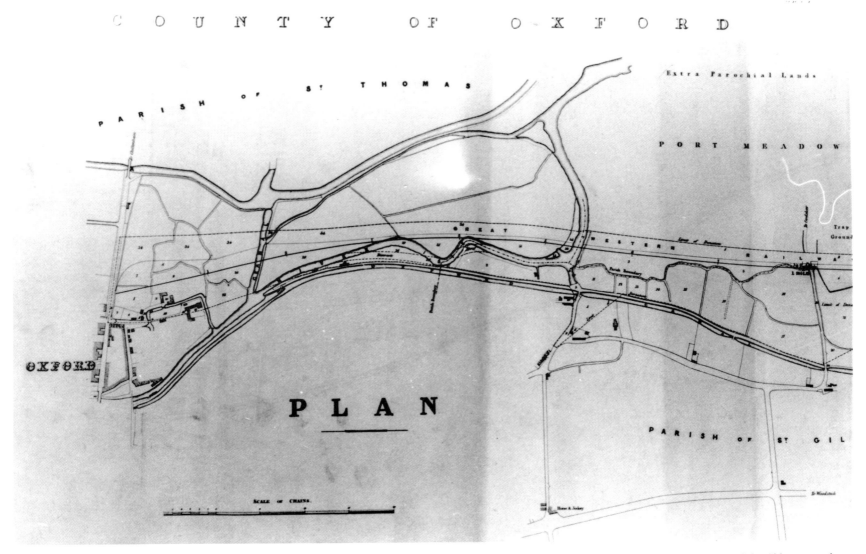

The ground plan survey by the engineers of the Buckinghamshire Railway at Oxford. Note the conspicuous water courses and the probable ruins of the Abbey near the road.

Oxford County Archives

One of the Precedent class of locomotives no 1213 *The Queen* about to depart from Oxford LNWR. As the locomotive was built and introduced in April 1892 and scrapped in February 1932 the picture could be anytime in the long time scale after 1905 as the new platform has been built.

L&GRP

After the closure of the station to passenger traffic occasional enthusiasts specials would visit as in this view in the late 1950's. Oxford based ex-GWR 2-6-2 tank no 6111 of the 61XX with a well stocked bunker is pausing for a tour of inspection.

Lawrence Waters

The view looking out from the platform in the late 1950's. The removal of the side screens gives a clear view of the look of the station, now handling only small goods and parcels and of course the busy coal yard.

The Station and Buildings at Oxford

The new Oxford station site was only agreed by the Board of the Buckinghamshire Railway in July 1850 and their Civil Engineer, Robert Benson Dockray was instructed to prepare plans, which he duly presented to the Board on November 7th, 1850, and the Board alloted £7000 for the building, with the resolution that 'the building be made and placed so as to be capable of extension without demolitions'.

The goods shed and passenger station positions were reversed to bring the passenger station nearer to the City.

The same day *Jackson's Oxford Journal* carried the advertisement for the opening of the new Banbury station so there also appeared the invitation for builders to tender for the construction of the new Oxford station

The Board met on December 12th to review the final plans and the Board Minutes read: 'in reference to the Central Station at Oxford. Mr Dockray produced plans shewing designs of the permanent buildings for both Stone and Wood Work. Resolved that Tenders be obtained for the Oxford Station on the plans proposed for the alternatives of wood and stone for the front of the buildings and also that Fox, Henderson & Coy be asked to tender for the whole of the erection on the plan of the exhibition building in all

respects, as information for the Board'.

Requirements of the specification were as would be expected with offices, passenger shed and platforms, goods shed, engine house, tank house, weighing machine house, carriage landings.

Tenders were submitted by January 9th, 1851, and the works were be completed by May 1st, 1851 (the same date that the 'Crystal Palace' was to open in Hyde Park, London.

Why were Fox, Henderson asked to tender for a different design to other tenderers? They were well known to the L&NWR Board. Fox having been a pupil of Robert Stephenson had worked on the L&B which became the L&NWR in 1846, and he had constructed the roof of Euston station in 1837.

As Henderson was present at Euston when the sealed bids were opened it is probable that the decision to appoint them had been taken in advance of the tenders being received, and as they submitted the lowest bid of £6552 for all the works, the Board called Henderson into the Board Room and informed him of the Board's decision.

'Resolved that the tender of Fox, Henderson & Coy be accepted as follows:- the whole works specified to be done for

£6552 including 12 months maintenance or if corrugated iron be used £31 more. Any alteration as to strength or detail, which Mr Dockray may consider necessary to be made at his request without increased cost to the Company. The whole to be ready for use in 3 months from January 16th instant. Mr Henderson accepted the Contract as stated in the above. With reference to the position of the passengers station, Captain Huish was requested to confer with the Engineer and on the ground to set out the station situation as may be expedient'.

There are no drawings on record of the other 18 schemes or tenders submitted and rejected and these would probably have been returned to the tenderers and are now lost or destroyed. The best that is known is that the Engineer appointed for the railway by the LNWR, Robert Benson Dockray (who was responsible for the design and for the supervising the construction of the Buckinghamshire Railway) described it as a stone structure. It appears to have been illustrated as something in traditional gothic with classical columns and a cast iron portico.

The Fox, Henderson solution followed the construction solutions utilised at Hyde Park as required by their tender invitation.

The use of iron and timber were common materials for the construction of railway stations and the LNWR station at Oxford would not seem to be in any way outstanding; unless of course one knows something more about its origins.

To the observant it has an almost austere and ascetic 'box shape' and therein lies the clue, that in its much reduced form it origins were in fact a part of something much larger by design, and this was the Great Exhibition building of 1851, constructed in London's Hyde Park described accurately as a 'palace of glass', the constructional scale of which the world had never seen before.

Added kudos for the Buckinghamshire Railway was that the station, no doubt gaily festooned with bunting could be opened as a gateway to the 'Great Exhibition' in a way that its GWR rival at Grandpont could not.

The side wall glazing was not included at Oxford, but the tongued and grooved vertical timber cladding replicated the Ground Floor of its 'parent' structure in London. Internally in the concourse area the walls were partially clad in galvanised corrugated iron.

Thomas Brassey had the contract for the construction of the line and civil engineering works, so it is likely that the Fox, Henderson works would have been confined to the buildings and incoming services. The swingbridge over the canal was therefore probably part of Brassey's contract as it is not mentioned in the schedule of buildings to be provided in the station building tenders.

Drawings have come to light of the Fox, Henderson & Co Oxford station building, site plans and goods shed building (many were presented to QRS by Railtrack when the building was being removed from Oxford) and it is probable that as soon as Thomas Brassey had completed the groundwork Fox, Henderson would have sent men from the Great Exhibition site to go to Oxford to carry out virtually the same working operations there, with the exception of the joining of the beams and roof trusses, which in the temporary Exhibition building were held together with Joseph Paxton's own design of hardwood wedge fixing. Fox, Henderson amended the design of the cast iron truss ends to take the traditional bolts. Oxford station was not planned for removal in six months, in fact it was intended to be very permanent and was dismantled only in its 148th year!

The Buckinghamshire Railway gained a real bargain. The goods shed was similarly constructed at a time when goods sheds were very much the poor relation in terms of station structures. Very often partially exposed which must have made them draughty places to work. More remarkable still was the water tank structure also in the same building pattern as the station. People travelling on the railway system in 1851 would certainly be impressed thinking that the Buckinghamshire Railway had presented itself in a very unique way at Oxford.

No pictorial evidence has come to light showing the appearance of the first 3 track engine shed, but it is probable that it followed the same cast iron construction as all the other buildings on site erected by Fox, Henderson, in accordance with their invitation to tender.

The board of the railway would be well aware of the publicity and revenue opportunities arising from the imminent opening of the Great Exhibition, and the tender documents sought to have the building ready to open on the same day as the Exhibition, but there were delays in negotiating the land purchase for the station site and hence the start date for the works.

Not all parts are successful in manufacture, which is in the nature of things, so there are always some rejected parts. Spoilage is something that every manufacturing company wishes to reduce and parts that may not be acceptable to take the weight of such a large structure as the 'Crystal Palace' , with its assembly of galleries would be perfectly adequate to take a single storey building at Oxford. But as we shall discover things can be taken to extremes.

Although Fox, Henderson confirmed an agreeable contract it has now been realised that they had used some cast iron columns that should have been rejected for use on the Station building. Time pressure from the start, but with the same completion date will have left no time in the construction programme for recasting of parts, so parts were used which in other circumstances would probably have been rejected. As late as April 10th the college had 'declined to part with property at Oxford', only 21 days before it was hoped to open the station! The station opened 6 weeks later, so there must have been a tremendous effort by the contractors once they got possession of the site.

Evidence can be seen of patch-up repairs being undertaken prior to despatch from the foundry in the decorative ironwork of the front elevation. Also evidence of 'cold shuts' in some columns where more than one crucible of molten metals had been used in a single casting and had partially cooled before the pour was completed, thus the joining edges of the two pours were different temperatures thereby leaving a crack in the casting.

The columns of the structure were used as drainpipes as they were on the Exhibition building.

The first excursion to the Exhibition run by the LNWR on the Bucks Railway was on May 1 the opening day and it ran from their temporary terminus at Oxford Road.

Rewley Road station opened on May 20 and an excursion from there on May 26 was on the first shilling day per head entrance fee to the Exhibition. The trip was scheduled to take $1\frac{3}{4}$ hours and cost 3 shillings and 6 pence ($17\frac{1}{2}$p) return and carried 400 people in new covered carriages. In the manner often experienced with excursions on the railway for many years after, it took much longer than the allotted time and took $2\frac{1}{2}$ hours. The GWR offered a rival excursion from their Grandpont station on the broad gauge at the same cost but scheduling $1\frac{1}{4}$ hours, they made much of their station at Paddington being nearer to the site at Hyde Park than Euston.

With the decline of the rail usage the GWR began to take over some of the LMS station responsibilities in the 1930's. An Act of Parliament in 1936 passed the swingbridge over to the GWR. It became scheduled as an ancient monument in 1976.

In 1958 the Western Region of the nationalised British Railways took over the entire Bletchley - Oxford route from about a mile east of Bicester on the 18 milepost.

After closure in September 1951 the station building was used as an enginemens' hostel until it was no longer required for this and was taken up by Regional Tyre Services as a tyre and exhaust fitting garage. In 1996 the tyre business left and the building was taken over by Budget Car Rental.

The Coal yard remained in use until the mid 1990's.

A cost comparison is interesting with Winslow and Bicester which were the two principle stations on the line, Winslow had to act as a junction station for the Oxford and Banbury lines for London trains as for some time the facilities at Bletchley were very poor. Consequently Winslow was built in brick in a twin pavilion style enclosing the portico entrance, but even then with low wooden platforms, all costing £4,879.

Bicester was built in the same style but in Oxfordshire limestone costing £4,800. Both stations had standard LNWR goods sheds which were probably added later.

At Oxford what appeared by staggering comparison was a 312ft train shed, with a 24ft port cochere, a very essential water tower and a commodious goods shed and engine shed for £7000!

The Crystal palace building was not originally designed for longevity, after the Exhibition was over it was removed, doubled in floor area and re-erected at Sydenham. It had inherent maintenance problems that proved financially crippling. A fire in 1888 destroyed some of the building and the remainder burnt down in 1936.

The Great Exhibition Building, the 'Crystal Palace' of 1851 from which the LNWR station at Oxford was an offspring. The building was 1850ft (564m) long, just over a third of a mile. It was 408ft(125m) wide at ground floor level and three stories high. The main transept was 72ft wide x 100ft high, to accommodate some trees that were on the Hyde Park site. The completed building had approximately 1,000,000 sq ft of floor area.

The characteristic view of the 'Palace' was the enormous glazed arch roof with its fan-vaulted ends. The decoration around the main walls found echoes at Rewley Road and the Port Cochere originally carried a similar fleur-de-lys decoration that probably disappeared with the re-roofing.

The 'Crystal Palace' was re-roofed in the 1880's, with the amazingly casual stance of the tradesmen posing for this photograph. From what has been deduced at Oxford it comes as no surprise that the original building had its problems on maintenance.

The centre aisle of the Exhibition provided space for the large exhibits where people could amply promenade at their leisure. In its immense scale it suggests the box like shape that the Oxford station was to be constructed to.

The galleries at the Exhibition showing the interior rigid structure.

The 'Palace' seen from the Serpentine bridge. The Tender of Fox, Henderson was accepted on July 26 1850, the contract was executed on October 31, 1850 though work had already begun with the first columns being fixed on site on September 26, 1850. The building was opened to the public on May 1, 1851 and closed to the public on October 15, 1851. Fox, Henderson had nearly every iron foundry in the West Midlands making parts for them and they were brought to Euston station by the LNWR. The parts were then hauled through the streets of London by powerful work horses to Hyde Park for erection.

The original 'Crystal Palace' type roof at Oxford with the 'ridge and furrow' running the length of the building. Drainage from the gutters was carried transversely to the columns that acted as drainpipes, an inherently weak arrangement with the bolt-holding column heads being doused internally with rain water. Note the low timber platform common to early stations. The rebuild came about 1905-6 and probably included the roof. The photograph has proved extremely valuable in supporting the view that the 'A' frames were added earlier, along with the extra roof bracing to give the structure added wind resistance which, in view of what has been learned of the structure on disassembly, was probably imperative.

The station with new roof and platform which is post 1906 with the introduction of the low elliptical roof bogie coaches of Wolverton replacing the earlier six-wheelers shown on page 24. Note the open area for ventilation just below the roof that was later fitted with timber louvered sections.

English Heritage

The Oxford station in 1935 when it was part of the system of the LM&SR. Note that the original vertical tongued and grooved timber cladding had been over-clad with horizontal tongued and grooved boards

A close up view of the entrance to the station yard in 1935, giving the only close view of the goods shed of similar structure to the station building. It was shared with the GWR as a result of a historic agreement between the one time Oxford, Worcester & Wolverhampton Railway and the LNWR, the former being absorbed by the GWR. Note the timber louvres just before the gutters.

The station came out of the war looking sadly neglected and apparently excluded from any further investment by the LM&SR who were inclined to to try to get rid of it to the GWR.

An ironic moment of celebration for the building at Oxford remembering the Great Exhibition one hundred years later with the 1951 Festival of Britain and shortly to close to passengers in the following September.

Great Western Trust

The ticket office at Rewley Road is believed to have been brought from the Great Exhibition after closure. Half of it also served as Stationmaster's office. The decoration around the roof edge is similar to that visible on a 1902 photograph of the station front. The crenellated decoration used externally on the 'Crystal Palace' was made from zinc.

The station and goods shed in the mid-1950's. In the foreground can be seen the standard LNWR timber goods shed added to the original one that is in the same design as the station itself.

The view looking from the swingbridge in the 1970's. On the left the stonemason's yard of Axtell, Perry & Symm. A large part of the station area had by this time been taken over for car parking space.

Bill Simpson

No photographic or drawing evidence has come to light showing the 3-road steam shed which had been part of the Fox, Henderson Tender remit. What however did survive until closure of the station was the water tank which was substantially supported with the cast columns as early tanks of this size normally required heavy brick built support. The two road steam shed visible is the one that survived to the end by F W Webb.

Photographs taken in 1970 when the station building had not yet entered its final phase of terminal decay. After serving as an enginemens' hostel the building was employed aiding road transport as Regional Tyre Services Ltd which lasted for another twenty years. The view is an obvious distorted amalgam of two prints but serves to show the front reasonably well.

Bill Simpson

The north-east side of the building in 1970.

Bill Simpson

Round-topped windows on the east side of the building disintergrated during dismantling and did not survive to preservation.

The back of the station building made into a hard standing area for a car park in 1970.

Bill Simpson

The east side wing from the front in 1970.

Bill Simpson

A view of the exposed columns and 'A' frames at the rear of the building in 1970.

Bill Simpson

On the right The west side in 1970 showing the original brick built weighbridge hut. Compare this part of the station building with the same side below in 1998. twenty-eight years of further deterioration is clearly evident.

The entrance to the station, 'modified' at some time by cutting through and removing a cast iron column support to increase the opening width for road vehicles during its use by RTS.

When this extension was demolished, it was found to have been built on the site of an earlier block, and original walls were still in place behind the 'new' construction. On one of the boards was a notice on how to trim lamp wicks. The was 'lost' during dismantling.

One of the huts occupied by local businesses at the station, this one by A A Robson Ltd.

Bill Simpson

From the back of the Coffee Tavern looking from the west in 1970.

Bill Simpson

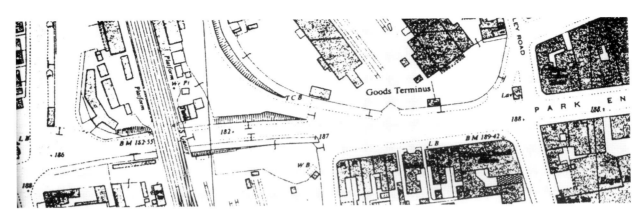

Oxford Transport Strategy and the Said Business School

The site had become very derelict with the passing years and an unrealised scheme of 1979 proposed a large hotel which would require to move the port cochere and the front of the building to an adjoining site integrating that into the hotel complex.

The remaining part of the station building was upgraded from Grade II to Grade II* in December 1985.

Oxfordshire County Council wished to re-design the road junction in front of the station area to free up traffic movement as part of the Oxford Transport Strategy. The implementation of the proposals would slice off the front half of the remaining part of the station building.

The Oxford Transport Strategy (OTS) was finally agreed following a bitterly contested public inquiry, but the inspector only dealt with the OTS requirements and specifically excluded the Grade II* station building from his award, leaving it to the parties wishing to carry out the development to make their case in respect of the station building and its future.

Had the OTS not been agreed, English Heritage would never have agreed to the removal of the station building.

The University of Oxford purchased the land upon which the station was standing in 1997 from Railtrack and wanted to remove the building.

The University proposed that the building be offered to a railway society. Such a proposal would have to be agreed by local planning authorities and English Heritage. They rightly expected that there would be opposition from local preservation groups as it would be removing a building of historic importance from the City, and over 50 letters commenting on the proposal were received from individuals and societies and a 4000 signature petition seeking its retention was received by the Oxford City Council.

If the building were to be removed it would therefore be

appropriate that its new location would have historic connections with railways that used the station - LNWR and LMS. Also that it would be within reasonable travel distance of Oxford and that public access would be available to the people that wished to see it in its restored form.

To this end the University assumed responsibility for the cost of dismantling, moving refurbishing, repairing, renewing and re-erecting the station building as there was no possibility that the old building would fit into their Said Business School plans for the site.

Quainton Railway Society appointed architect Lance Adlam to carry out a feasibility study for locating the building at the Buckinghamshire Railway Centre, and to review what alterations would need to be made to the building to accommodate the Society's requirements.

The building was offered to a number of interested organisations, and Quainton Railway Society Ltd were keen to have the building as their new Visitor Centre for the Buckinghamshire Railway Centre and could offer the building long term security on the site as they own the freehold of the land, which satisfied English Heritage's requirements. It was the most appropriate location as the building would not be far from the original Oxford site.

Following a meeting with the QRS Executive Committee and the Surveyor to the Oxford University the Society was offered the building and Lance Adlam was invited by the University to act for them and QRS as a joint client. Oxford University provided the funds for the movement of the building and an endowment towards the cost of future maintenance.

A scheme for reconstruction at Quainton was prepared and received planning permission from Aylesbury Vale District Council, following which an application for Listed Building Consent was made to Oxford City Council to demolish the station building.

The University Surveyor appointed the rest of the specialist consultancy team during this period to commence the pre-contract works. Gifford and Partners of Southampton were appointed to a number of roles: structural engineers, building surveyors and archeologists; Ridge (Oxford) were appointed as cost consultants and Quantity Surveyors; Jessop & Cook were appointed as Planning Supervisors, and Silcock Dawson & Partners were appointed as services consultants.

Listed Building Consent was eventually granted with a long list of conditions attached, all of which had to be resolved before any dismantling works could proceed and these are shown in the next chapter.

During this period of negotiations the squatters from the A34 Newbury Bypass were evicted by the Under-Sheriff of Berkshire and settled in the derelict station building as a new home and made the proposed removal of it their new cause celebre, even though they quite obviously knew nothing at all about the building!

Their occupation gave the 'protesters' media coverage and eventually the Under-Sheriff of Oxford arranged their removal from the building with his counterpart, the Under - Sheriff of Berkshire (who knew most of the protesters by name having evicted them from the Newbury Bypass site!) and with police support and a surgeon in attendance with his bone saw in case anyone chained themselves to the structure which would require a surgical operation to remove them by cutting through their limbs! The 'protesters' had no sympathy for their cause from the authorities, who knew them for what they were. Removal commenced on 'Battle of Britain' day, but 47 years later, on September 14, 1998.

Once free of the protesters, the site was fenced and a 24 hour manned guard was installed, with some large dogs which discouraged the uninvited 'guests' from returning, and allowed the serious work of measurement and recording of the structure to begin.

By agreement with Oxford City Council, the University arranged for the roof coverings to be removed in November 1998 so that the building was rendered uninhabitable, on the understanding that if planning permission and listed building consent were not granted, then the University would have to reinstate the roofs.

Oxfordshire County Highways poster illustrating plans for development of the area.

OCC

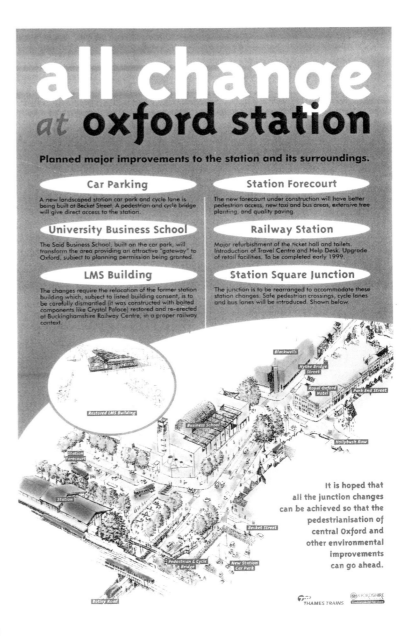

all change *at* oxford station

Planned major improvements to the station and its surroundings.

Car Parking

A new landscaped station car park and cycle lane is being built at Becket Street. A pedestrian and cycle bridge will give direct access to the station.

Station Forecourt

The new forecourt under construction will have better pedestrian access, new taxi and bus areas, extensive tree planting, and quality paving.

University Business School

The Said Business School, built on the car park, will transform the area providing an attractive "gateway" to Oxford, subject to planning permission being granted.

Railway Station

Major refurbishment of the ticket hall and toilets. Introduction of Travel Centre and Help Desk. Upgrade of retail facilities. To be completed early 1999.

LMS Building

The changes require the relocation of the former station building which, subject to listed building consent, is to be carefully dismantled (it was constructed with bolted components like Crystal Palace) restored and re-erected at Buckinghamshire Railway Centre, in a proper railway context.

Station Square Junction

The junction is to be rearranged to accommodate these station changes. Safe pedestrian crossings, cycle lanes and bus lanes will be introduced. Shown below.

It is hoped that all the junction changes can be achieved so that the pedestrianisation of central Oxford and other environmental improvements can go ahead.

THAMES TRAINS   OXFORDSHIRE

The GWS 6998 'Burton Agnes Hall' on a special
in 1992 seen from beyond the swingbridge.
Bill Simpson

5 Planning and Listed Building Consent – Conditions

Oxford City Council granted Listed Building Consent for application 98/0058/L on November 12, 1998 which is consent to demolish. To secure the future of the building there were 10 conditions attached to the consent which had to be complied with prior to any dismantling work starting on site. The requirements are paraphrased for brevity below:

Condition 1: Work to commence within 5 years: standard condition.

Condition 2: Work to conform to 7 statements accompanying or added to the application, including the planning approval by AVDC for the building to be erected at Quainton.

Condition 3: Building to be carefully dismantled for reconstruction. Works to be supervised by the applicants' archaeological contractor (recorder), structural engineer and architect. Below ground parts to be recovered for re-use at Quainton unless English Heritage agreed otherwise (they did agree otherwise following inspection of the parts by their structural engineer).

Condition 4: This consent shall not be implemented until a continuous building contract is in place, which provides for careful dismantling of the former station building in Oxford and for its immediate transfer and reconstruction at the Buckinghamshire Railway Centre at Quainton Road, Quainton, Bucks, as given planning approval by Aylesbury Vale District Council and as indicated on the submitted drawings (document statement 4).

Reason: To avoid doubt and to ensure a programme of works that avoids any delay or storage of the dismantled building and as sought by the English Heritage Commission. (English Heritage recently had another scheme: a seaside pier that had been taken down and then the parts were put into store, with no requirements to rebuild it!)

Condition 5: Consent shall not be implemented until a contract for a full and detailed above-ground archaeological and photographic recording survey is in place, ...to record the former station building as it now is and to record and subsequently publish, the history of the fabric (including earlier roof forms) as this is revealed and destroyed by the process of dismantling.

Condition 6: Archaeological recording of the below ground works before construction could start on the new Said Business School

Condition 7: This consent shall not be implemented until a contract acceptance letter has been sent to the successful contractor for the Highway works at Park End Street proposed by Oxfordshire County Council, which involves the land presently occupied in part by the LMS station.

Reason: As consent to demolish this Grade II* listed building is exceptional and should proceed on the full understanding that the highway junction alterations are about to commence and as sought by the English Heritage Commission.

Condition 8: Repeat of Condition 1

Condition 9: One month's notice shall be given to the Royal Commission on Historic Monuments for England, National Monuments Record Centre.............. before any work commences on site.

Reason: To allow RCHM to carry out their own survey. (Following discussions with the architect RCHM didn't wish to carry out their own survey and a copy of the Gifford Archaeological report has been filed with them).

Condition 10: The Local Planning Authority through Planning Control and Conservation shall be kept fully informed............ and 7 days notice of the start of works on site to be given.

Reason: To ensure compliance with conditions and to provide an opportunity for inspection of the works by the LPA. The Oxford City Council Conservation Officer and the architect were in weekly contact with occasional site meetings to ensure that this condition was met.

As can be seen there was a lot of work to be carried out in a very short time to get all the conditions complied with. The most important from the QRS viewpoint were Conditions 3, 4, 5 and 7. Oxfordshire CC were pushing hard for the building to be removed quickly and yet they were the last piece of the jigsaw to be in place so that we could start works.

At the date of the granting of the LBC Gifford's archaeologist, surveyors and structural engineers were already working on compliance with conditions 3 and 5; Condition 4 was in place with contractors Jesse Mead of Chesham and their specialist dismantling contractor - St Blaise; Condition 9 had been dealt with, and a start was made on site on December 7, 1998 at Oxford and the new car park at Quainton which was necessary as the Rewley Road station building was to be re-erected on the existing car park site.

Survey and Dismantling at Oxford

Gifford's surveying team took measurements of the building to allow the future archaelogical studies to be located and the archaeologist also commenced recording the existing structure in October 1998. One important level that was taken was rail level in relation to the concourse floor level. There was a buffer stop with a short length of connected rail that allowed the correct datum to be set for the reconstruction works. Unfortunately the drawing of the station building did not come to light until after the works were completed. It would have been very useful to have had it earlier, as it clears up a number of previously unexplained matters.

When the dismantling work began and the archaeological recording started in earnest the remains of earlier constructions indicated that the building had a fairly chequered history and had been subjected to a considerable number of changes. A certain amount of historic study of old plans and the Ordnance Survey maps and other desk studies revealed interesting changes that had taken place within the building and the archaeology was showing where and how some the changes had been implemented.

The 'A' frames and intermediate trusses were installed (c. 1888) before the building was fitted with a new roof which is proved by the earliest known interior photograph of the station on page no 24 (pre-1906).

If you look at the added structure at Quainton, the new trusses spanning off the 'A' frames are deeper than the originals and the addition of knee braces stabilises the frame assembly as a virtual portal frame. The 'A' frames were tied longitudinally to the original trusses adjacent to the existing column heads with an angle section and also by the introduction of diagonal bracing at truss top flange level, thus creating a high level stiffening of the roof support layer, without the new structure actually supporting the roof vertically. The assumption is that the original structure proved to be inadequate for resisting the wind loads put on it by the side cladding and the structure was strengthened by the 'A' frames, trusses and ties. As the new structure was not apparently providing vertical support to the original roof, why else would it have been installed under the new roof with all the disruption to the station working that would have been involved?

In February 1975, James Sutherland wrote an article for *The Structural Engineer* (see appendix) comparing the structures of the Crystal Palace with Rewley Road station and he referred to a drawing that seems to have disappeared with time (reference: drawing no 66792 LNWR Oxford Passenger and Goods Station: July 1888) which refers to the A frames being a new construction.

Reference to drawings of the building now in the Quainton archive show that the goods shed had a similar roof construction and that it also had similar 'A' frames and trusses added.

The original trusses top flanges were drilled for fixings at 8ft centres, to coincide with the longitudinal gutter positions, which were supported above the top flange at the node point where the struts supported the flange, all as you would expect. The longitudinal gutters supported the ridge and furrow roofs and spanned the 24ft between the original trusses. The furrow gutters discharged their rainwater into secondary transverse gutters that spanned across the building supported on the trusses. They discharged this rain water into the cast iron columns which also formed the rainwater pipes. This construction arrangement with the 'ridge and furrow' roof glazing was exactly the same as used on the Crystal Palace.

The 'A' frame trusses top flanges were not drilled at these 8ft centres positions, where they could have provided support to the longitudinal gutters, though the top flange was level with the top of the existing trusses and therefore their introduction provided no vertical support to the original roof.

The 'A' frames were constructed from used permanent way rail as pressure marks are clearly evident where they had been fixed to chairs whilst in use on the line. They have the dates rolled into the flanges for 1868 and 1872 at Crewe Works and allowing for time spent as part of the permanent way, it is believed that the 'A' frames were probably erected in 1888, as noted above. The drawings showing the reconstruction of the roof, turning it at 90 degrees to its original span, in the form that it is now on the re-erected structure, show the roof to have been re-designed in 1905-6 which would coincide with the general upgrade of the line, including raising the platforms all along the Buckinghamshire Railway line, for the introduction of the new bogie coaches. The 1906 drawing shows that the new glazed roof was omitted above the line of the two tracks so that the loco steam and smoke would vent directly outside.

The original platform level was approximately the same as the concourse with old 4 and 6 wheel coaches having two footboards to get up into the carriages. The later coaches had one footboard close to the platform level, as raised. A copy of a plan recently discovered showing the 1906 proposed alterations shows a change in the ramp up to the platform level with an easing of the slope from 1:7 to 1 : 17. At the top of the ramp there was a short level section and a fence and gates to form a ticket barrier. The concourse level was originally built of timber boards and joists on brick cross walls. The area was filled and concreted with the c.1906 works to the roofs and platforms. The side blocks retained their suspended timber floors to the end, though some areas had subsequently been filled and concreted on the west side.

Within the building enclosure the new raised platform had a 2½ inch (65mm) concrete topping whilst outside, the platforms had 2½inch concrete flagstones. The whole platform length had 3ft wide x 4 inch thick hard York stone non-slip edging to both sides.

The quality control on many of the castings used at Oxford was appalling, though the science of metallurgy was in its infancy. The 'circle in a rectangle' panels to the front elevation and port-cochere were out of square and many were broken and had been repaired at the factory before being incorporated in the works. Note that as these are non-structural they have been reused on the re-erected building as they are part of its history.

Some columns included 'cold shuts' (as noted before in chapter 3), where the melt had not properly run around the whole column section, despite the liberal use of phosphor to improve the melt fluidity. The use of phosphor has of course added its own problems with its different cooling characteristics to the grey iron introducing the lamina failures within the castings and increasing the fragility of an already slender column. The columns had several castings with defects with wall thickness, where the core armature has obviously not been accurately centred, or has dislodged during casting.

The old column heads have been incorporated into the new works as the concourse end balustrade columns at the end of the platforms and the variations in walls thickness can clearly be seen at the bolt holes.

The 16 ft long (4.877m) main columns stood on 8 foot long (2.439m) base columns, which stood on a lump of concrete. There was no degree of fixity for the columns at ground level and the concrete pads appeared to be standing on the original flood plain at natural ground level, so the columns were only restrained by the made up ground. This probably accounts for the variations from the column grid location that we found on our pre-dismantling survey and would doubtless have added to the stresses within the grey cast iron frame.

The 24 foot length of column and base combined would have probably been too much for the slender 8 inch diameter cast columns. In the extension at Quainton we have used modern steel Circular Hollow Section (CHS) columns to satisfy the current building codes and have introduced knee braces to match the 'A' frames.

The original trusses have all been re-used. Apart from removing a rivet and inserting a larger bolt, the original design satisfies the current codes of practice. Repairs have had to been carried out where the weather has attacked the structure and replacement of some castings that were found to be broken, probably during manufacture, where the cold castings were hot rivetted to the rest of the frames causing the cast iron to crack.

The July 11, 1906 drawing of the station building with the proposed new roof also notes that "Further instruction will be issued with regard to the re-boarding of the side(s)". The side walls originally had two large doors and a lifting section in the platform. Outside were two wagon turntables. The doors would allow the transfer of wagons from one side to the other (goods yard - station - coal yard) without the use of a locomotive. Much wagon movement on early stations was carried out using 'shunting horses' as locomotives were in short supply and needed for train haulage work. Shunting horses were finally phased out in the 1960's with the end of the Railway's 'common carrier' responsibilites and the 'smalls' traffic that they had to carry. Added to this was the introduction post war of the Scammel 'Mechanical Horse' and the Lister Motorised Trolley

It is believed that the original 3 track engine shed was built in the same manner as the station, as was the goods shed. The engine shed was replaced in the 1880's with a new standard LNWR Webb designed 2 track shed with a 'saw tooth' roof profile.

The water tower by the engine shed was supported on cast iron structure that owed its origins to the Crystal Palace designs. It is likely that the columns were cast with thicker walls to support the weight of the water in the tank above, and reference to the available photographs shows the cast iron columns at 8 ft centres, rather than the 24ft grid used in the main building.

A handsome cast iron port-cochere was constructed at the station entrance. It used parts in common with some areas of the building and some special new castings. This was already missing when the building was dismantled in 1999.

The inherent problems of poor maintenance did affect the Oxford building, most significantly the additional strengthening brought about by the 'A' frames and an entirely new design roof which was built in the Edwardian period between 1906 and the start of World War I.

There are some interesting parallels in the station building with the construction of the Crystal Palace and these are covered in James Sutherland's article. The column shafts on the Oxford building are 16ft long whereas on the Exhibition building they were 18 ft 3 inches, but they are the same diameter. The side walls are thickened where necessary to carry the imposed loads.

The truss spans at Oxford covered 48ft, exactly as used in parts on the Crystal Palace.

In contrast with the Crystal Palace where Paxton used his design of a patent hardwood wedge fixing on the columns to secure the trusses, the Oxford trusses of both patterns have swellings in the end castings to take bolt holes and the columns were joined to the trusses with long through bolts which passed through the rainwater outlets, with the inevitable consequences of deterioration.

There has been some speculation as to whether the bolt fixings were to avoid a Paxton patent, or were a Fox, Henderson response to a building that was designed for greater longevity and permanence than the original Crystal Palace.

Conclusions of the Gifford report were that evidence was found of cutting corners with patching and painting of columns to hide blow holes and other imperfections from the casting process. The evidence all pointed to a rush job using less than satisfactory component parts, not at all as the Great Exhibition building promoting British engineering innovation and excellence. The delayed start on the site and the reduced construction programme would support this view.

Dismantling of the building and all the items to be recovered were delivered to Quainton by April 9, 1999, and the station site was handed over to the Oxfordshire County Council Highways Division and to the University of Oxford for the commencement of their works for the Said Business School.

A final view being a composite photograph assembled by Lance Adlam looking from the Blackwell building prior to the start of dismantling.

The sub-surface column supports removed from the ground to reveal that the drainage down the columns was piped from the side with points at the top on some and at the bottom on others; the bottom being the large disc base that rested on a concrete pad. Consequently some would have wet rotting residue filling up to the drainage point. The bolt ends are of course where they were fastened to the columns.

Lance Adlam

The ending of an era, the station shortly before the process of disassembly began.

The characteristic of the 'Crystal Palace' design is the circle in the rectangle, beneath which are the arches between columns. A number of these had been cast too thin and fractured which was concealed with remedial work of plates being bolted over fractures. Also some of the joining lugs did not line up, and were bodged to fit. Note the pin hammered through in the centre. One wonders how such obvious defects escaped the eye of the inspecting engineer of the LNWR, certainly R B Dockray who was the Chief for the region had a reputation of having an assiduous eye, proved by his inspections during the constructions of the railway. Or perhaps he was encouraged to look the other way!

Lance Adlam

A view inside the building at Oxford, note the non supporting wooden columns between the arches that now serve as entrance to the refreshment area at Quainton. The structure on the left were the offices for Regional Tyre Services Ltd.

Lance Adlam

Amongst the final photographic views at Oxford of the station being removed with the new Oxford station on the line of the former Great Western Railway in the background.

Lance Adlam

Progressive survey and recording work was carried out at Oxford during disassembly with Gifford Archaeology and St Blaise for refurbishment and re-erection. This view is the west side lower block roof (over current cafe).

The buffer stops and rail that gave the relative levels between the track and the concourse, that became buried in subsequent infill, returned to the light of day. This well reinforced structure was likely to have been put in by the LMS to replace some old LNWR timber ones that had probably deteriorated. The buffer has been recovered and is now at Quainton. Note the 'Crystal Palace' type roof trusses on the ground behind with their lateral strengthening fitted ready for transport off-site.

Lance Adlam

What looks like apparent chaos at Oxford as a heavy duty lifting crane removes part of one of the west side block roof trusses. But out of this came the Said Business School and a re-designed road junction area.

Lance Adlam

Looking across station site.

Lance Adlam

METALLURGICAL ANALYSIS.

We have obtained metallurgical analysis of the column EC12M1. As expected, the phosphorus level is very high (outside the range of the spectrometer!) which means that its tensile strength will be below 140N/mm2. with very low strain before failure.

Carbon	3.41
Manganese	1.11
Silicon	1.85
Sulphur	0.08
Phosphorous	>1.5
Nickel	<0.005
Chromium	0.03
Molybdenum	<0.005
Copper	<0.005
Tin	0.008
Titanium	0.04
Vanadium	0.07

See following page for Test Certificate. (CSL Laboratory services).

Up to the beginning of the century, the techniques had not been developed to achieve high molten metal temperatures from the cupolas used at the time. For sufficient fluidity to run the thin walled castings the level of phosphorous eutectic Fe3P which permiates the cooling iron finally setting at 950 degrees centigrade. However, because of the contraction of Fe3P differs from the other constituents, fissures are set up weakening the structure.

Spectrographic analysis.

Courtesy of F. J. Thornton

Damaged column.

Lance Adlam

Quainton Road Station and
The Buckinghamshire Railway Centre

A few miles away from one of the stations that once existed on the Oxford - Bletchley line, Verney Junction, is the station of Quainton Road. This station was a creation of the same men that promoted the Buckinghamshire Railway so a historical link exists there.

In the early 1860's Sir Harry Verney and a number of other landowners in the district became dissatisfied by the delays and second fiddle treatment of the LNWR. This company had not yet quadrupled and rebuilt its 1838 main line which was under severe pressure from lines that had joined it bringing much extra traffic. Yet the LNWR would not support a new line from the Buckinghamshire Railway going through Aylesbury and joining it at Harrow.

The Duke of Buckingham and Sir Harry Verney did at

last prevail upon them to accept a line from Claydon to Aylesbury, to link up and work with the existing Aylesbury branch. This was in 1860, but in the following year the austere and supremely practical character of Richard Moon became chairman of the LNWR. Moon was not a man of 'arrangements' made by the Duke whom he had succeeded. When an obstructive publican at Aylesbury was asking too much for his land and business Moon seized on it to abandon the scheme linking across Aylesbury, even though some construction had begun.

The Aylesbury & Buckingham Railway, as the new line was called, had received the Royal Assent on August 6, 1860 and work began from the Claydon end in February 1861, but it would take two further Acts to raise the capital required which was made difficult by an investment crisis in 1866. It would require this difficulty to be overcome before the line was finally opened in 1868, and then came the blow from Moon.

As a consequence of Moon's decision the board of the A&B company had a railway with no connection at Aylesbury, and one set of points connecting to the Oxford - Bletchley line at Verney Junction. The LNWR had now become hostile to the small company and its link line of some twelve miles. Stations opened were not the most accessible, Quainton Road about a mile from the village and just as remote were Grandborough Road, Winslow Road and Verney Junction.

Salvation when it came was from the arch rival of the LNWR - the GWR, who had promoted The Wycombe Railway from Maidenhead to High Wycombe, Princes Risborough and to Thame, eventually to Oxford. From Princes Risborough they threw off a branch to Aylesbury. It is tempting to imagine that this was to spite the LNWR.

The GWR had gone through some trials after their track gauge of 7ft was not adopted by the country at large which was settled on a 'standard gauge' of 4ft 8½ins. Consequently they had to accept the inevitable and convert their tracks from broad to standard gauge. It was very useful for the Aylesbury & Buckingham that the GWR chose in 1868 to make that change on the line to Aylesbury upon which they could then run standard gauge stock through to the Aylesbury & Buckingham, an agreement that the A&B were anxious to conclude.

The line was not a success with only three trains each way daily and the LNWR refusing to accommodate them on its Oxford - Bletchley line with poorly timed connections.

When in the 1890s the Metropolitan Railway guided by Sir Edward Watkin showed interest in the A&B line they were keen to exact a good bargain to sell it to them. The LNWR were now facing someone with greater muscle power at Verney Junction and the time of Sir Richard Moon had already ended.

The Metropolitan Railway formed a Joint Committee with the Great Central Railway that had extended as the Manchester, Sheffield & Lincolnshire Railway from the north. In consequence the stations were all rebuilt as much more substantial structures in the early years of the twentieth century. The two stations of Grandborough Road and Winslow Road remained remote on the line to Verney Junction, but Quainton Road was now on the new main line to the north and south to London. The Duke of Buckingham died in 1889 and Sir Harry Verney in 1893, so although they did not see it, their original plans for the Buckinghamshire Railway had at last been realised.

Quainton Road remained therefore as not only a principal station but also the junction station for both the Verney Jct line and the Tramway of six miles to Brill. This was a creation of the Duke opened by him in 1871-72 but closed by the London Passenger Transport Board in 1935. They had adopted the rights of the Joint Committee in 1933. The section from Quainton to Verney Jct was closed in 1936.

The other partner to the arrangement of the line, the GCR, became part of the LNER who continued to run the main line services after the grouping of the railways in 1923.

British Railways took over on January 1st, 1948 and implemented their modernisation schemes culminating in the 'Reshaping of British Railways' report by Lord Beeching in 1962. The former GCR main line was included for closure which took place in 1966 when the track was lifted from Claydon Junction northwards and singled from Claydon Jct to Aylesbury.

Two years later, the London Railway Preservation Society was formed and Quainton Road station was eventually taken over for preservation.

One of the authors remembers visiting in the thin chill of a Winter's day in 1968, when a sprinkling of snow covered the ground and a line of stock and industrial locos stood, some sheeted, needing rescuing from rusty oblivion on one of the sidings. The Society members were rightly warming themselves with tea in the building on the Brill branch platform.

LRPS later became the Quainton Railway Society Ltd and there must have been many buckets of sweat and some anguish to restore locomotives and stock, let alone burning frustration in struggles with various authorities. So it should be said that much is owed to the efforts of people like the Society members, both at Quainton and in all the other enclaves of restoration in the country that work so hard so that the young can still see something of the great steam age.

It is now the Buckinghamshire Railway Centre and in the peaceful area of countryside one can visit, observe, ride, and take afternoon tea in the new visitor building in a haven of contemplative relaxation.

The site for the building that was agreed to be at the Buckinghamshire Railway Centre at Quainton was the former car park area and this brought some very heated controversy within some members of the Society over the correct orientation of the train shed with rail access looking towards the bridge abutment and not open to the yard, as it would have been as a station as some members wished to reinstate it.

Quainton Railway Society did not want the building to be used as an open station with trains running into it and creating dirt in the process, but wanted it to become their new Visitor Centre for which they needed the pedestrian entrance to have easy access from the new visitor car park.

Railway vehicles are able to access the platform via a traverser at the rear. In its new location, the former Oxford Station has greatly enhanced the amenity of this major museum of railways.

The site at Quainton pre-preparation, the building was to go on the ground covered by trees in the centre of the photograph. The station of Quainton Road is on the right.

Lance Adlam

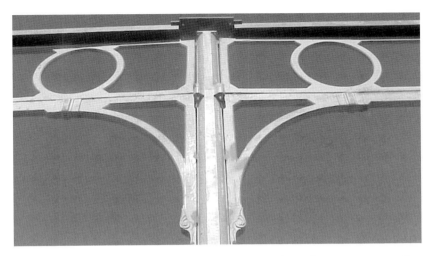

Reconstruction and Extension

Following receipt of all the timber and non-ferrous parts at Quainton, or of the cast iron parts to F J Thornton, an ironfounder in Wolverhampton, and the wrought iron trusses to a specialist sub-contractor in Ellesmere Port by April 9; came the subsequent delivery of the dismantling record drawings and schedules. There then followed a massive exercise by the architect and contractor in sorting and evaluating the condition of approximately 20,000 scheduled parts that were stored on site.

Working drawings were prepared for the re-erection of the building with much time spent in cross-checking items and dimensions with the stored parts.

The major timber elements were repaired or manufactured in a temporary woodwork shop set up in one of the Romney units, another Romney was racked out for storage and part of a third one was used to erect and repair the 2 side block roofs of what are now the Cafe, Oxford Room and the Shop and Offices.

The new 'up' side car park was completed on March 23, 1999 (and was put to good use for the very wet Easter weekend events) which cleared the site for the re-erection of the station building.

A temporary office building was acquired through the contractor and located in the new car park to form the temporary entrance to the site for all visitors and this was later acquired by QRS from the builder, resited on the 'down' side and is currently (2007) used by the Chief Engineer.

Reconstruction work on the 'new' station site commenced on the 'Glorious Twelfth', August 12, 1999. This began with the removal of the railway carriage that had formed the

QRS offices and site entrance for staff and visitors, together with moving a small group of coach bodies that had been used as sales outlets for groups on site.

The many castings required were manufactured by F J Thornton of Wolverhampton. There were 5 new columns, 19 new pattern column bases with rainwater outlets and 13 new column heads. During the repair works required to the trusses several of the end castings that bolt to the column heads and a couple of the cruciform struts had to be replaced as they were also broken, as noted before. All the new castings were made in ductile iron to eliminate the fragility of the original grey iron work.

By November 20, 1999 the ground floor slab, foundations and drainage were all completed and the first 2 columns were erected on their new bases together with their new column heads, and on the 25th, the first truss was lifted into place. The station iron work had all been erected by December 15, 1999 ready for the scaffolders to erect the 'birdcage' scaffold to prepare for the next phase of the works to start in January 2000. The building proved its worth to some of the Society's disbelievers as December 2000 was a very wet period and the building provided shelter for all visitors, except for the short dash to the trains!

Phase 2 Extensions: 2001

QRS had a small committee referred to in the Quainton News No 86 as the 'Gang of Four', which comprised of QRS Chairman, Andrew Bratton; Curator, Roy Miller; Sales & Marketing Manager, Allan Baker and architect, Lance Adlam, who were dealing with the whole scheme of the site development, and had made an application for a grant to the National Heritage Memorial Fund who agreed to provide funding of £1,225,000 to extend the station after re-erection, with five extra bays to the rear and the replacement of the porte-cochere at the front restoring the building to look like the original station at Oxford. An additional grant was given of £530,000 to complete the works.

Also included in the funding package was the provision of the new traverser that gives stock access to the station, the improvement of the site access routes, including a new footbridge over the Railtrack/Network Rail line that bisects the Buckinghamshire Railway Centre. The refurbishment of the unique Cinema Coach and the implementation of a site wide educational and information strategy was an important part of the Educational and Public Access requirement of the grant.

Works commenced on January 4, 2001 on the extension of the building, with a new contractor appointed: Latimer Contracting, and they completed the works to the building at the end of July 2001 ready for the tracks to be laid into the building.

The 'New York' coach was moved on August 10. It should have been moved earlier but the crane caught fire at Wing on its way to the Centre and melted the road surface making recovery very difficult!

The foundations and traverser rails were completed and levelled on a very cold November 15 and the traverser arrived on a large lorry on November 19 to be installed on the same day and commissioned by November 27.

By January 22, 2002 the building had a Great Western Railway locomotive and a number of carriages installed by using the new rail link siding and traverser.

Arriving in an entirely different setting, the restored building on site at Quainton with the village visible in the distance.

Lance Adlam

The newly repainted structure with the start of the new roof and by all accounts a much better structure than it was originally!

Lance Adlam

'New' Porte-cochere structure under erection. There was only one photograph of the original to guide us on the design.

Lance Adlam

A view made possible by the new footbridge at Quainton, the railway station that would not die, but has a successful new lease of life to be enjoyed and admired hopefully for another 150 years! This photograph was taken very early in the morning before sunrise as soon as the footbridge had been fitted into position. Note: Chris Jenkins by platform.

Lance Adlam

Sir William McAlpine, President of the Quainton Railway Preservation Society unveils a plaque and addresses the meeting at the official opening ceremony. Alongside him, on his right, is Andrew Bratton Chairman of the Society. It was the culmination of prodigious effort to secure from an almost hopeless situation a lasting representation of the railway age at Oxford.

Lance Adlam

An external view of the station on the official opening day with appropriate Oxford City road transport from different periods.

Lance Adlam

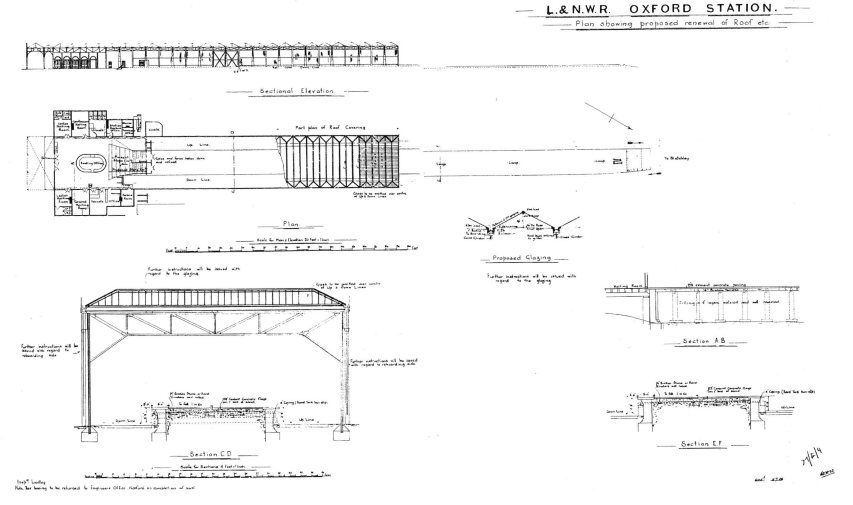

L.& N.W.R. OXFORD STATION.

Plan showing proposed renewal of Roof etc

Sectional Elevation

Part plan of Roof Covering

Plan

Proposed Glazing

Section A.B

Section C.D

Section E.F

British Railway Journal

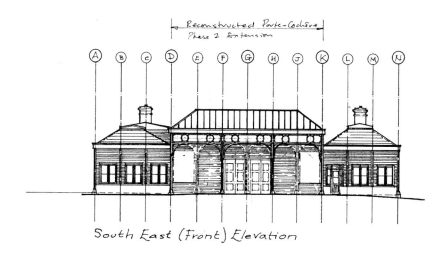

Reconstructed Porte-Cochère
Phase 2 Extension

Ⓐ Ⓑ Ⓒ Ⓓ Ⓔ Ⓕ Ⓖ Ⓗ Ⓙ Ⓚ Ⓛ Ⓜ Ⓝ

South East (Front) Elevation

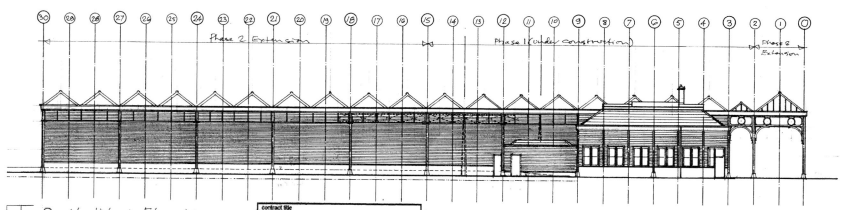

㉚ ㉙ ㉘ ㉗ ㉖ ㉕ ㉔ ㉓ ㉒ ㉑ ⑳ ⑲ ⑱ ⑰ ⑯ ⑮ ⑭ ⑬ ⑫ ⑪ ⑩ ⑨ ⑧ ⑦ ⑥ ⑤ ④ ③ ② ① Ⓞ

Phase 2 Extension   Phase 1 (under construction)   Phase 2 Extension

South West Elevation

KEY PLAN

contract title

BUCKINGHAMSHIRE RAILWAY CENTRE

Phase 2

This is a drawing that was prepared for Phase 1 of the works and that is reissued for the Phase 2 extension contract

Lance Adlam ATP RIBA
CHARTERED ARCHITECT
6 Salisbury Close
Princes Risborough
Buckinghamshire HP27 0JF
Tel & Fax   01844 345423

contract
Resiting Rewley Road Stn.
at Bucks Railway Centre
drawing title
Elevations

drg. no.
77/22
scale
1:200
date
2/4/98

Phase 2 - Transhed Extension

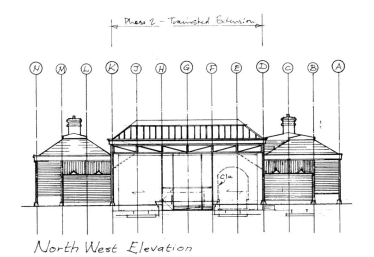

Ⓝ Ⓜ Ⓛ Ⓚ Ⓙ Ⓗ Ⓖ Ⓕ Ⓔ Ⓓ Ⓒ Ⓑ Ⓐ

C1a

North West Elevation

Note: Existing platform and Rail levels to be verified by further archaeological investigation.

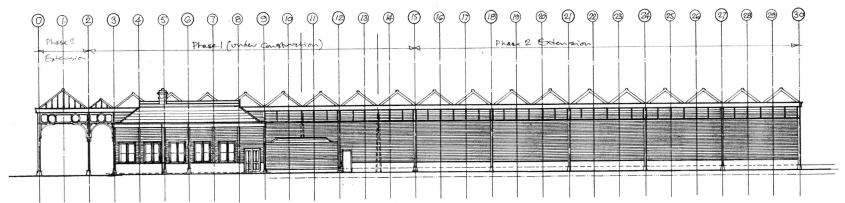

⓪ ① ② ③ ④ ⑤ ⑥ ⑦ ⑧ ⑨ ⑩ ⑪ ⑫ ⑬ ⑭ ⑮ ⑯ ⑰ ⑱ ⑲ ⑳ ㉑ ㉒ ㉓ ㉔ ㉕ ㉖ ㉗ ㉘ ㉙ ㉚

Phase 2 Extension

Phase 1 (under construction)

Phase 2 Extension

North East Elevation

KEY PLAN

contract title

BUCKINGHAMSHIRE RAILWAY CENTRE

Phase 2

This is a drawing that was prepared for Phase 1 of the works and that is reissued for the Phase 2 extension contract

Lance Adlam ATP RIBA
CHARTERED ARCHITECT
6 Salisbury Close
Princes Risborough
Buckinghamshire HP27 0JF
Tel & Fax   01844 345423

contract
Resiting Rewley Road Stn at Bucks Railway Centre

drawing title
Elevations

drg. no.
77/23

scale
1:200

date
2/4/98

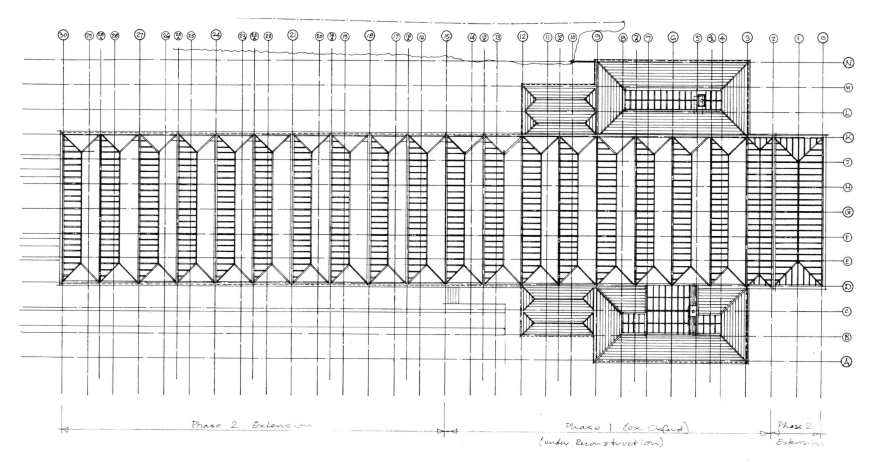

Phase 2 Extension   Phase 1 (ex. Oxford)   Phase 2
(under Reconstruction)   Extension

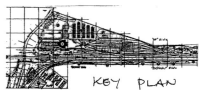

KEY PLAN

contract title

BUCKINGHAMSHIRE RAILWAY CENTRE

Phase 2

This is a drawing that was prepared for Phase 1 of the works
and that is reissued for the Phase 2 extension contract

Lance Adlam ATP RIBA
CHARTERED ARCHITECT
6 Salisbury Close
Princes Risborough
Buckinghamshire HP27 0JF
Tel & Fax   01844 345423

contract
Resiting Rawley Road Stn.
at Bucks Railway Centre

drawing title
Roof Plan

drg. no.
77/21

scale
1:200

date
9/4/98

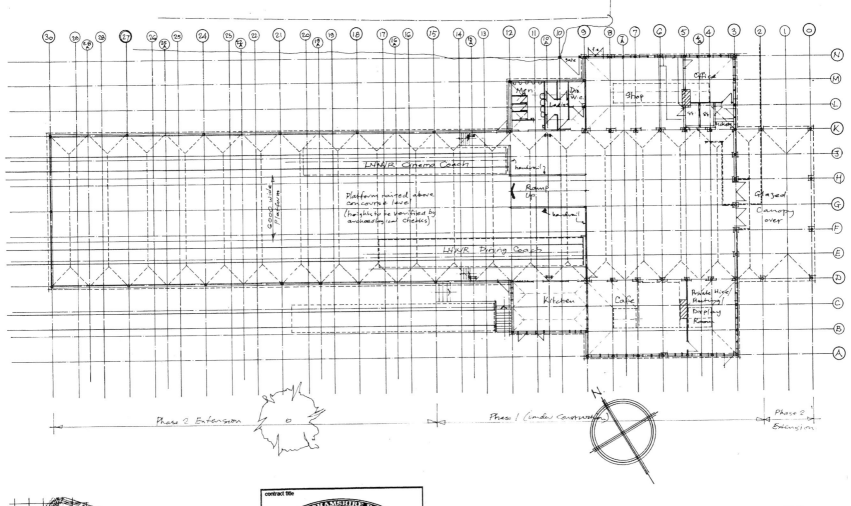

LNWR Cinema Coach

Platform raised above concourse level (heights to be verified by archaeological checks)

Good wide Platform

LNWR Driving Coach

handrail

Ramp Up

handrail

gate

Men

Ladies

Dis. W.C.

Office

Shop

Kitchen

Cafe

Private Hire / Meeting / Display Room

Glazed Canopy over

Phase 2 Extension

Phase 1 (under Construction)

Phase 2 Extension

N

KEY PLAN

contract title

BUCKINGHAMSHIRE RAILWAY CENTRE

Phase 2

This is a drawing that was prepared for Phase 1 of the works and that is reissued for the Phase 2 extension contract

Lance Adlam ATP RIBA
CHARTERED ARCHITECT
6 Salisbury Close
Princes Risborough
Buckinghamshire HP27 0JF
Tel & Fax   01844 345423

contract
Resiting Rawley Road Stn. at Bucks Railway Centre

drawing title
Floor Plan

drg. no.
77/20

scale
1:200

date
2/4/98

Appendix: James Sutherland

UDC 624 (091)

Oxford Midland Station and the Crystal Palace

by R. J. M. Sutherland, BA, CEng, FIStructE, FICE

Harris & Sutherland

The Institution's Special Study Group on the History of Structural Engineering intends to promote short articles on subjects of historical interest for publication in The Structural Engineer as a fairly regular feature.

Dr. Norman Davey's paper 'Roman concrete and mortar' published in June 1974, was one such article. As a contrast to 2000 year old concrete, Mr. Sutherland turns, in the paper below, to 19th century iron, and compares the surviving remains of the Oxford Midland Station of 1851 with the drawings and other records of its contemporary, the Great Exhibition Building.

Fox Henderson & Company built both and the similarities are so remarkable that it could almost be said that the Crystal Palace still survives, at least in part.

In spite of all that has been written on 19th century construction, and about the Great Exhibition building in particular, records of the Oxford Midland Station are tantalizingly sparse. Thus there are not only gaps in this comparison but there is evidence, again incomplete, of conscious changes of mind or perhaps of a lack of unanimity amongst the designers of the Exhibition Building. Any further information—even conjectures—would be welcome. It is the aims and reasoning of our predecessors which are valid for us today even if some of their techniques are now superseded.

Until recently it had been thought that no trace of the Crystal Palace structure remained. Strictly, none does, but something very similar has survived. Henry-Russell Hitchcock was perhaps the first to draw attention to this[1] in the early 1950s when he wrote:

'There at Oxford is an extant sample of the original Crystal Palace construction as authentic as the great monument at Sydenham which burnt down in 1936'.

He was referring to the Oxford Midland Station, originally part of the Buckinghamshire Railway, then of the London and North Western and now abandoned and half demolished but with the remaining wedged fixings used in the Exhibition Building (Figs 2, 3 and 4).

Superficially, the Oxford Station—a simple rectangle with a single span of 48 ft across the tracks and columns at 24 ft centres longitudinally (Fig 1)—does not look much like either the Hyde Park Exhibition Building of 1851 or the same building as re-erected at Sydenham. In spite of this even a quick comparison of the components shows that the buildings are at least very closely related.[*] The column castings are the same in all but their shaft length. The cast iron lattice edge beams at Oxford are identical to the standard 24 ft cast iron floor beams for the Exhibition Building in every detail except the end fixings, the Oxford beams presumably being made from the same pattern altered only enough to substitute a pair of bolts for the famous wedged fixings used in the Exhibition Building (Figs 2, 3 and 4).

While the 24 ft cast iron beams look the same, the main 48 ft wrought iron trusses at Oxford do not at first seem much like the equivalent spans for the Exhibition Building. At Oxford these are of the Pratt type with tensile diagonals only whereas in the Exhibition Building each panel was counter-braced (Fig 5). Closer examination shows this refinement to be illusory, in that the redundant compression diagonals in the Exhibition Building were not structural at all, but of wood. Introduced, as Downes and Cooper explain, 'merely . . . to preserve the uniformity of appearance of the truss'[2]; that is to make them look similar to the cast iron ones. In the station this refinement was omitted but continuous top and bottom flange plates were added. Virtually all other details are the same except that as with the cast iron beams the wrought iron trusses at Oxford are bolted at their ends instead of being fixed with wedges.

[*]This comparison is made possible by the survival of the working drawings of the Exhibition Building superbly reproduced in Downes's and Cooper's book of 1852.

The Structural Engineer/February 1975/No. 2/Volume 53

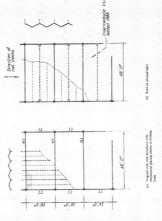

Fig 1. Framing plan of train shed at Oxford

Almost more telling as a comparison than the structural components are the remains of the decorative iron cladding at Oxford which was clearly made from the same castings as in the Exhibition Building. (Fig 6).

Despite minor differences, and to date a lack of firm written evidence, the similarities between the components are such that it seems inconceivable that the buildings could have been built by different people. Certainly the dates tie up: the Great Exhibition Building was opened on 1 May 1851 and the Oxford Midland Station less than three weeks later on 20 May. One contemporary newspaper report refers to the station as 'constructed in a similar manner to the Crystal Palace in Hyde Park' and to Mr. Fox's presence at the opening[3]. This is presumably Charles Fox (later Sir Charles) of Fox Henderson and Company but it would be reassuring to find a fuller reference, especially as 'Thomas Brassey (also present) was the contractor credited[4] with the construction of the Buckingham Railway and not Fox Henderson.[**]

Fuller details of the contractual arrangements at Oxford would be interesting. We know that the Exhibition Building was strictly a contractor's alternative the credit for which must be shared between Paxton, who initiated the scheme, and the tenderer, Fox Henderson and Company, who proposed it; the design split is hazy but there is no doubt that all the

[**]The engineer is variously quoted as Robert Stephenson and Dockray; it is likely that both were involved.

69

In February 1975 James Sutherland wrote an article for The Structural Engineer pointing out the relationship between the Great Exhibition building of 1851 and the Midland station at Oxford. Much of Mr Sutherland's observations have in succeeding years been confirmed and we reprint here the illustrations that he used for further enlightenment and in recognition of these early observations made by him, with his kind permission and also that of the Editor of the *Structural Engineer*.

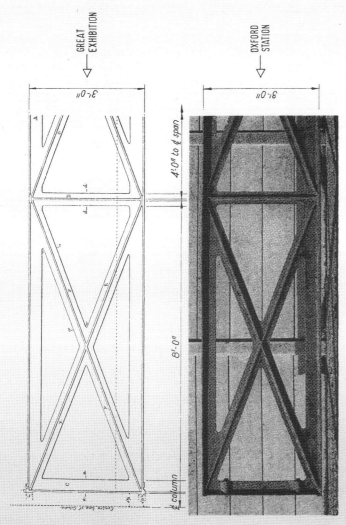

Fig. 2. Comparison of 24 ft cast iron beams

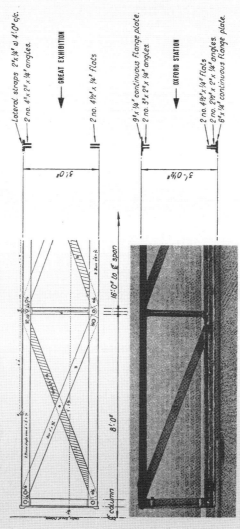

Fig. 5. Comparison of 48 ft wrought and cast composite trusses
(Note: non-structural timber diagonals in Great Exhibition trusses shown cross-hatched)

detailing and the whole structural analysis were done by Fox Henderson. Was the Oxford Station again an alternative or did the tender inquiry for the line give only an outline specification for the stations? Were there any other stations as closely related to the Exhibition Building, either on the Buckinghamshire Railway or elsewhere? It seems not but one cannot be sure.

This paper is frankly an interim statement full of questions which others may help to answer. Perhaps even more interesting than the purely factual uncertainties are the doubts on design and intention.

There can be little doubt that the station was the child of the Exhibition Building and not the other way round but it is noticeable that the station was not just knocked up out of the left-overs from the larger contract. The differences point to distinct changes of mind. Were the flange plates to 48 ft trusses at Oxford added for extra bending strength (the load seemed to have been nearly enough the same in both cases) or because the Exhibition ones lacked stiffness laterally, especially during handling? Were the bolted end connections—much sounder to the modern mind—adopted because the original wedging proved less easy and less secure than

77

Fig 4. Beam to column connection in Great Exhibition Building

24 ft between the iron trusses as at the Crystal Palace. The holes in the tops of the trusses are quite compatible with this idea. With poor maintenance, of which there is ample evidence, the gutter beams might well have rotted between 1851 and the 1880s and leaked or even collapsed, after which the whole roofing was changed. If this conjecture is correct it is surprising that the same trouble did not occur at Sydenham in the much longer period until the fire in 1936.

Two complete bays from the demolished part of the structure (six columns, three trusses and four cast iron beams) have been taken into the Science Museum store and it is hoped that there will be a structural gallery in the museum some day large enough to accommodate them. It would then be appropriate to reconstruct a section of the glazing, if only we knew its form. Any photographs or drawings of the station before the changes in 1888 would be more than welcome. If these showed that Paxton gutters were used so much the better. What is more, this type of roof covering would be comparatively easy to reconstruct.

References

1. Henry-Russell Hitchcock, *Early Victorian architecture in Britain*, 1954.
2. 'The building erected in Hyde Park for the Great Exhibition of the Works of Industry of all Nations 1851. Illustrated by twenty-eight large plates, embracing plans, elevations, sections and details laid down to a large scale from the working drawings of the Contractors, Messrs. Fox, Henderson & Co', by Charles Downes,

71

Fig 3. Beam to column fixing at Oxford Station

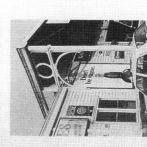

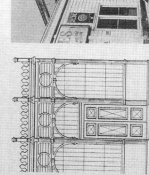

Fig 6. Comparison of decorative cast iron cladding sections
Great Exhibition Building   Oxford Station

the published accounts indicated, or was the wedging Paxton's idea which Fox never liked?

Finally what was the original roof covering at Oxford and why was this altered in 1888 when the present crude intermediate frames were introduced which halved the secondary spans and probably altered the direction of glazing. The only surviving drawings which British Railways can provide is dated July 1888 and shows these intermediate frames as new but not what the roof covering was like before. It is at least likely that the original glazing ridges ran longitudinally with Paxton type trussed timber gutter beams (Fig 7) spanning

Architect with scientific description by Charles Cooper, Assoc. Inst.CE. John Weale, 1852.
Note: a reprint of this has been issued recently by the Victoria and Albert Museum.

3. *Jackson's Oxford Journal*—Saturday 31 May, 1851.

4. Sir Arthur Helps *Life and labours of Mr. Brassey*, 1872.
   Charles Walker, 'Thomas Brassey' *Railway Builder*, 1969.

5. Drawing No. 66792 L&NWR Oxford Passenger and Goods Station: July 1888.

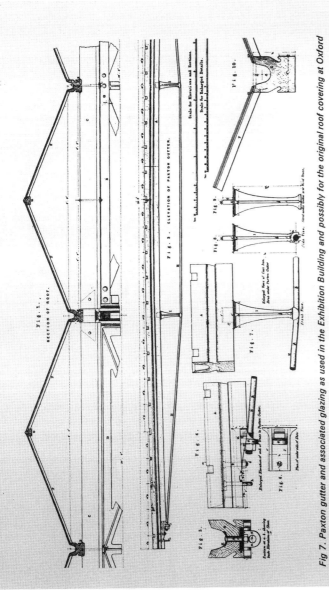

Fig 7. Paxton gutter and associated glazing as used in the Exhibition Building and possibly for the original roof covering at Oxford

Acknowledgments

Phase 1 Works - Removing the Building from Oxford and reconstruction at Quainton

Joint Client
The University of Oxford and the Quainton Railway Society Ltd

Architect and Project Manager
Lance Adlam Chartered Architect (Princes Risborough)

Structural Engineer, Building Surveyors and Archaeologists
Gifford & Partners (Southampton)

Quantity Surveyor
Ridge and Partners (Oxford)

Building Services Engineer
Silcock Dawson and Partners (Princes Risborough)

Planning Supervisor
Jessop and Cook (Oxford)

Building Contractor
Jesse Mead (Chesham)

Specialist Dismantling and Recording Contractor
St Blaise

Ironfounders
F J Thornton (Wolverhampton)

Car Park and Access Road (at Quainton))
Richard Ashford Ltd (Aylesbury)

Phase 2 Works - Extension of the Building and other Site Works at Quainton

Funding of the Works
The National Heritage Memorial Fund (The National Lottery)

Client
The Quainton Railway Society Ltd

Architect and Project Manager
Lance Adlam Chartered Architect (Princes Risborough)

Structural Engineer
Gifford and Partners (Southampton)

Quantity Surveyor
Ridge and Partners (Oxford)

Building Services Engineer
Silcock Dawson and Partners (Princes Risborough)

Planning Supervisor
Graham Jessop (Oxford)

Building Contractor
Latimer Contracting Ltd (Tetsworth)

Ironfounders
F J Thornton (Wolverhampton)

Traverser Manufacturers
Mechan Ltd (Sheffield)

New Footbridge and Access Paths
L G Kimber Engineers (Brill)